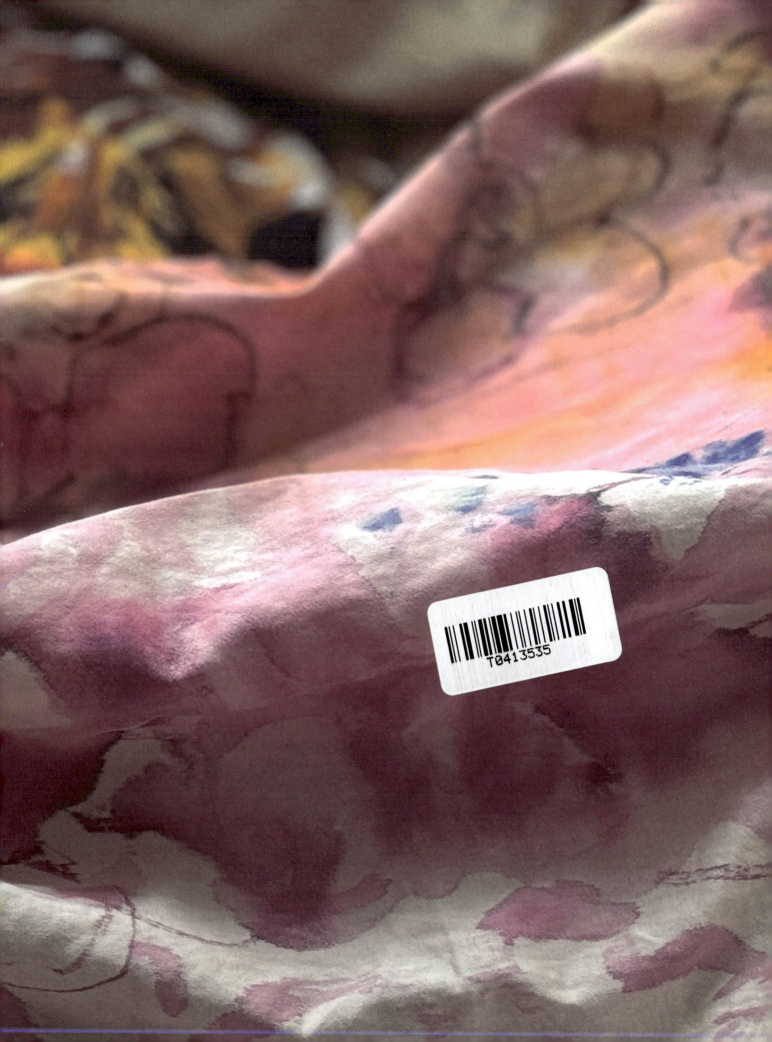

An Artist's Journey

tinystories

Tiny de Vries

TERRA

my journey

5 hi, its me

6 Indonesia
back to Bandung

30 The Netherlands
house, atelier and city

70 Morocco
Atlas Mountains, Sahara, coast and Marrakesh

152 Germany
atelier Morgentau

168 Australia
Tasmania, Bruny Island, Daylesford and Melbourne

214 France
the south of France, the Dordogne

254 my favourite places

256 made with love

hi, it's me

Where do I begin to share my story, to reveal the essence of who I am and what I do? Each page of this book is a reflection of my soul, revealing my pursuits and my inspirations. Join me on this journey where I recount my life as an artist. Let me inspire you, share the beauty in the mundane and encourage you to stand still, observe, marvel and feel.

From a young age, I knew that my destiny was intertwined with the arts and that I wanted to go to the University of the Arts. My childhood was a canvas, and my family painted it with vibrant colours of art, freedom of expression, and exploration of the world. Our home was a playground of imagination, where we tended to our garden, sewed and dyed our own garments, went to ballet lessons and acting classes, and played the piano. We drew and painted every day. My sister and I were exposed to the beauty of the world through visits to museums, exhibitions, and the studios of my parents' artist friends. My fondest memories are of the Kröller-Müller Museum in Otterlo, where I spent hours admiring the art. Our family vacations were always spent on the Wadden Island of Ameland. Life was carefree and full of light until I turned sixteen and lost my beloved sister, my other half. The world lost its light for me but my father said: "Tiny, choose the light. Celebrate life." He gave me a coin and said: "Go out and explore the world and if you ever need me, use this coin to call me and I will come and pick you up."

and that was what I did, I chose the light and spread my wings

Upon completing my studies at the University of the Arts, Utrecht, I embarked on a journey to Indonesia. My time in Bandung, on the island of Java, proved to be a transformative experience, shaping me both as an individual and as an artist. I was a timid dreamer back then, but my mentor in Bandung saw something in me and urged me to express my innermost thoughts and feelings and tell my story through my art.

In my atelier, Tinystories, I weave a world of optimism and poetry through my paintings and collages. My muses are the beauty of nature, flowers, landscapes, the figures and faces of women, the allure of travel, and the mystique of Asia. I find beauty in the ephemeral, in the imperfect, in the frayed edges of things. Each new piece is accompanied by a verse, a small story told in paint. My art is an extension of my heart, my love, and my soul. Each piece is a visual poem, a delicate reflection of emotion, a dreamy narrative.

Art is a journey, and every journey has a story. This book is a window into my world, an invitation to join me on my journey as an artist. So come along, take my hand and let us travel together on this journey!

With love,

x tiny

Indonesia

back to Bandung

opening my eyes and heart

Chop chop chop. As I stir from my slumber, the familiar symphony of breakfast, or lunch, or maybe already dinner being prepared, greets me. In this country the whole day is devoted to preparing and eating food. The birds are chirping in the background, and I hear Elina's dulcet tones along with Alfonzo's slightly warmer timbre. Outside, the hum of mopeds, the splashing of water and the lively calls of street vendors add to the vibrant cacophony. A gentle breeze blows in through the open windows caressing my skin and sending a shiver down my spine. A new day has dawned. Ten minutes later, I find myself seated with a steaming bowl of rice and vegetables before me. Elina pours herself a cup of tea. Aldhira, the eldest son, has made coffee especially for me. The elderly house cat brushes against my bare legs causing a tickling sensation that brings a smile to my face. I feel content, as if I am right at home.

Three months – that's how long I should have stayed, but fate had other plans in store for me and I ended up staying several years. As a student at the University of the Arts in Utrecht I had arranged a place at the art school in Bandung, never imagining what lay ahead. "Go for it! Indonesia is beautiful," my father said. Oh, my father! He sent me out into the big, wide world, telling me he would always be there for me. Perhaps this is why I am so fearless? And so I went with visions of Indonesia as a land of sandy streets with white art deco buildings and tropical greenery. Reality proved different.

As I step off the train in Bandung, I am met with an overwhelming cacophony of noise and dirt. I walk past one cheap hostel after another, drop my rucksack at one of the hostels and go in search of a phone box, as this was a time before mobile phones. I call Alfonzo from the post office. When I hear his voice, I breathe a sigh of relief. "Just come on over to our house, you are truly welcome," he says. I take a taxi to a completely different area of the city where I finally see the historical houses of my imagination. Most are shabby with vines and foliage entwining the crumbling walls.

Alfonzo and Elina's beautiful old abode is a white stone house, its huge roof protruding beyond the walls to form a shady veranda. Inside, the ceilings are high and cool brown tiles provide respite from the heat. A cooling breeze blows through the slatted windows. A large palm tree stands proudly in front of the house. Out back in the courtyard garden, tall trees and tropical plants vie for attention. The prominent durian tree is the great pride of Elina's mother, she will tell me later. Nestled at the rear of the garden lies a low building which serves as a residence for students and bustles with activity. Solitude is an alien concept here.

I feel content, as if I am right at home

Alfonzo and Elina reside with their two sons and Elina's mother. Two aunts live here too. I remember the cosy afternoons when the house was filled with the chatter of Elina's mother and her friends as they converse in a mix of Indonesian and Dutch and drink tea with homemade *bokkenpootjes* – a traditional Dutch biscuit.

My stay here is a profound odyssey that was forever to leave an indelible imprint on my soul. I embrace the adventure with open arms. Within two months with the help of Elina's mother, I have mastered the language reasonably well and I feel more at one with the people here. In my mind I am one of them. But Alfonzo chuckles at that. "You smell of cheese," he teases. In those early days at their home, he introduces me to a world of new flavours. Together we venture to the market to buy fresh fruit, and each day I discover more about the Indonesian cuisine and savour new delicacies. They beam with pride when I exclaim excitedly at the rapturous tastes. After two weeks, the scent of cheese I exuded is but a distant memory.

In no time at all I find myself woven into the fabric of Alfonzo's family. We journey together, visiting their artistic circle and creating memories. They, in turn, become my family. As the years pass, the bond becomes stronger. Adhika, their youngest son, will live with me for three months when he is in the Netherlands for his internship, and my children have now become good friends with the two children and are in almost daily contact. Our bond is unbreakable – a testament to the power of family and friendship.

we journey together, visiting their artistic circle and creating memories

I startle from my reverie over my bowl of rice with the realisation that I have to leave for university and work on my graduation project – an album about a woman who practices Jamu, a traditional Javanese medicine. This herbal drink, passed down from mother to daughter, boosts the immune system with its secret recipe. I accompany her on her early morning rounds through the kampung's narrow streets as she visits her clients. I photograph her, make screen prints and paint her portrait. Though I learn much at the academy, it is here, among the people, that I truly grow. We lift each other up, helping each other instead of competing. I flit from class to class, immersing myself in the world of art and local crafts.

The next day, I accompany Elina to her friend's batik workshop. My heart sings as I wander through the vibrant space. Batiked fabrics and exquisite ikat cloths flutter on long lines, their intricate patterns mesmerising me. I marvel at the craftsmanship on display. From a young age I have always been enamoured with all kinds of fabrics. I collected them, treasured them and even began sewing my own clothes from self-dyed fabrics at the tender age of twelve. My love for embroidery knew no bounds as I painted with thread creating wild, untamed patterns. No neat cross-stitches in a predetermined, regular pattern for me.

I watch, entranced, as Elina's friend applies hot wax to the fabric with a metal stamp. This ancient technique of batik where the paint doesn't stick to the waxed sections thus creating intricate design calls to me. How I long to learn, to perfect the art. I imagine I would need to come here every day for a year to learn batik to perfection and to be able to design my own stamp patterns. For now, I am content to watch and listen to Elina converse with her friend. To be inspired. That afternoon, I paint orchids in the colours of the batik fabrics. Deep purple, aubergine, brick red, and a smidgen of white.

Elina and Alfonzo, a university lecturer, are sources of knowledge and inspiration. They open my eyes to the wonders of art, crafts, history, and the intricacies of life. Alfonzo inspires me, urging me to express my own stories through the strokes of my paintbrush. Together, we visit the studio of a friend of Elina's where paper is made from the banana tree. The threads of the trunk are ground and chopped into pulp, mixed with water and glue and shaken out in a sieve to release the water. The sheets are then laid out in the sun to dry. They turn what is essentially waste, into beautiful paper. I purchase an array of sizes and colours of this banana tree paper and

later take it to Emmy's castle in France where I create my own paintings.

Elina is a ceramist. She runs her own ceramics studio where she teaches her craft. One summer we had the pleasure of making mugs in her studio. Working with her was an absolute delight. The clay, sourced from Sukabumi, had a beautiful hue. We experimented with a variety of homemade glazes, creating tones in shades of brown, red, and dark green, reminiscent of the warm landscapes of Java.

The Javanese people have a deep connection with nature and a rich history of craftsmanship. They use the resources available to them to perfect their craft with love and devotion, creating truly beautiful works of art.

The work I create in Bandung overflows with love. Love for this land, its nature, and its people. Smiles greet me at every turn. Here, I learn the unspoken rule of not touching, but offering a smile as a gesture of warmth instead. Beauty surrounds me. Clothed in my kimono, I wander the streets in the early morning light, plucking fragrant frangipane flowers. Their sweet scent fills my senses. The locals greet me, and I strike up a conversation with two women strolling down Jalan Mangga in our shared language of Indonesian. They reveal the secret of finding the best blooms – by reaching for the overhanging branches. Verdant plant tendrils weave their way through the urban landscape as plant cuttings sprout from halved plastic bottles. The lush greenery creeps up to the doorsteps. I meander through the streets making my way to the yoghurt shop I frequent. The plentiful stalls lining the streets are a testament to the resilience of the people as they strive to make a living in a world that isn't always kind. I see it all and I know – life here is a beautiful struggle.

I am often inspired to capture the essence of Javanese women in my paintings. Their gentle gaze, always accompanied by a warm smile, exudes serenity and modesty. Yet, beneath this calm exterior lies a strength and determination that is evident wherever I go.

As an artist, I revel in the chaos of creation. My palette is a riot of colours, each hue vying for attention in a sea of trays and old sheets of paper. I am drawn to the texture of handmade paper and India ink and like to make collages using these. My painting 'Follow Rivers' is a testament to this process – a portrait of a woman, her visage emerging from a collage of sheets and colour. The name is a reflection of my approach to life, one that embraces the unexpected and revels in the unknown. I experiment with paints that shouldn't work together, watching as they clash and melt in unexpected ways. I leave my work unvarnished, allowing the colours to fade over time until only the black of the ink remains. To me, this is where the magic lies.

smiles greet me at every turn, as a gesture of warmth

Bandung holds a special place in my heart, a place where I know I will always be embraced with open arms. It is a home away from home where I am surrounded by the warmth of family. For family is the foundation of everything and in Bandung I am blessed to have found mine.

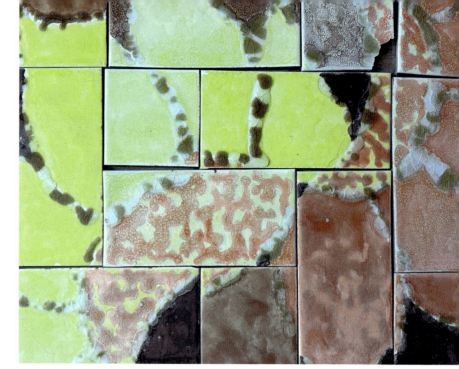

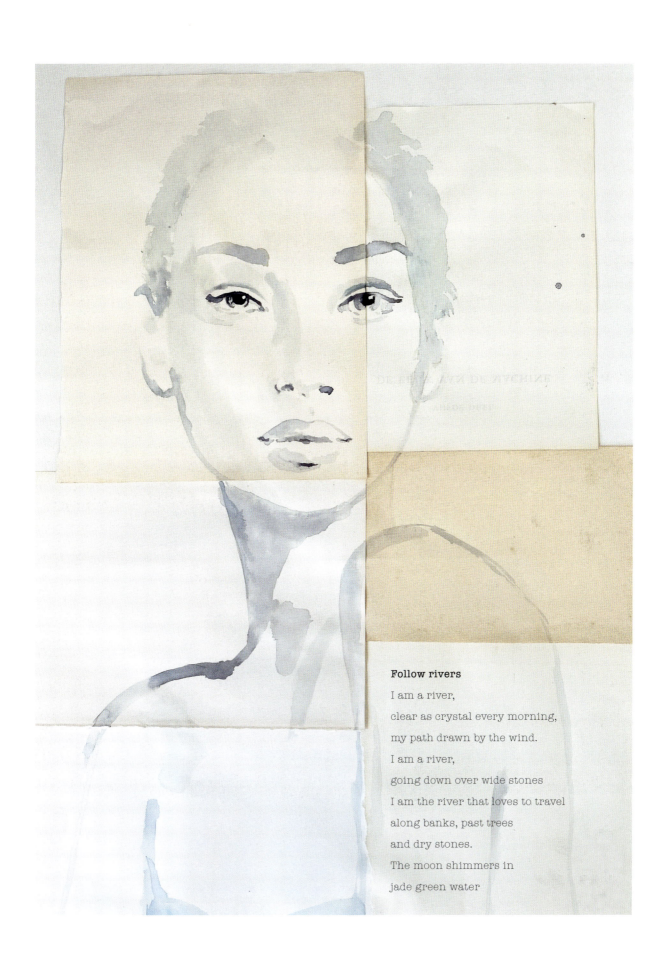

Follow rivers

I am a river,

clear as crystal every morning,

my path drawn by the wind.

I am a river,

going down over wide stones

I am the river that loves to travel

along banks, past trees

and dry stones.

The moon shimmers in

jade green water

The Netherlands

house, atelier and city

this is home

With a gentle push I open the towering doors of my French balcony. The sweet melodies of birds, chirping and singing in harmony heralding a new day, emanate from the garden. I pause, closing my eyes, and bask in the warmth of the sun on my skin. It is one of the first days of spring and the air is crisp and invigorating.
I wrap my kimono snugly around me, ready to embrace the beauty of the day ahead.

It was ten years ago that my husband and I first set foot in this abode in the city of Utrecht. I wandered through the rooms with their high ceilings, captivated by the arched windows in the bedroom, the intricate woodwork, the fireplaces in each room, the dark wooden floors.
I knew: this is it. Light poured in from every direction, illuminating the space. To me, light is essential in a home. As we ascended the stairs, we entered a beautiful, luminous room. I knew immediately that this was to be my studio. French doors opened onto a roof terrace revealing a breathtaking panorama of the city. I looked around and smiled. We had found our home.

I paint deep into the night in my studio. The stillness of the darkness outside envelops me, and I cannot bring myself to stop. My studio is my sanctuary, an island of creativity. As I paint, my thoughts ebb and flow like the tide, sometimes crashing like waves, other times gently lapping at the shore. It is in these moments that inspiration strikes, and I can visualise the paintings I have yet to create taking shape in my mind.

When I paint, I prefer to sit on the floor with all the different creations I am working on spread about me. My materials are at the ready – paper, trays of vibrant paint, brushes, water, and oil pastels. Dried flowers, cotton, linen and old books add texture and depth to my creations. I sometimes reach for past drawings and paintings from my chest of drawers, drawing inspiration from them or incorporating pieces into new collages.

Painting is an intuitive process for me. I like to experiment with unconventional tools such as twigs, homemade pencils and Japanese brushes. I prefer to work on antique linen or aged paper, thinly layering diluted paint or ink to achieve a transparent, dreamy, poetic effect. The unexpected is always welcome, as the paint spreads and reacts in its own mysterious way. I embrace the small imperfections and uncontrolled lines, finding beauty in the balance between finished and unfinished. It is a tribute to serendipity, and I revel in the process. I amble towards the kitchen with the thought of brewing a cup of coffee in the traditional Moroccan style – *nous nous* a perfect blend of half coffee and half milk. I pour the steaming concoction into one of my handmade ceramic mugs.
As I settle down amidst the cushions by the open doors, I take a moment to survey my surroundings. My gaze falls upon the large sofa in the front room, where we often spend our evenings, nestled close to each other, while our feline companion, with its fiery red fur, lounges lazily in the big armchair.

The low benches on the garden side were crafted by a skilled carpenter, as was the dining table. These benches are versatile, serving as seats, loungers, and even makeshift beds for guests. My own artwork adorns the walls, while a stack of art books supports a floor lamp. Its lampshade, decorated with dried wildflowers, casts a gentle, soothing light in the evening. I have a passion

our house is filled with love and memories – recollections and mementos of moments passed

for heirlooms, vintage furniture, memorabilia, and small-scale handmade treasures, each with their own unique character and history. My collection, gathered from near and far, is artfully arranged in small vignettes, telling stories through their still life compositions.

My passion for textiles and layering is evident in everything I create. From ikat to block prints, velvet to jacquards and batik, my fabric collection is an eclectic mix from all corners of the globe. I love to experiment with prints and patterns, creating unexpected combinations that somehow simply work. I drape them over chairs, tables and sofas. A delicate, embroidered tablecloth from Vietnam doubles as a curtain to keep out the summer heat. And my weekly trips to the fabric market in Utrecht never fail to yield a new treasure, whether it be a piece of fabric to paint on or to turn into cushions.

I was born in the small, quaint town of Elburg, a medieval town, which, like Utrecht, is nestled in the heart of the Netherlands. When I was a child, my family and I moved to a bungalow on the outskirts of the old town designed by my uncle, an architect like my father. Our home was a beacon of light, with its large windows and sliding glass doors that opened up to a sprawling, wild garden. Inside, my father's studio and my mother's atelier were sanctuaries of creativity, while the light wooden floors added warmth to our home. My mother's large paintings adorned the white walls. We dined at an antique table, passed down from my great-grandparents, surrounded by Marcel Breuer's Wassily chairs in natural leather. A Kho Liang Ie sofa and a light-wood sofa with oversized homemade linen cushions provided comfortable seating, while stacks of architecture and home magazines served as makeshift side tables. First-time visitors often expressed surprise at the sparse furnishings and lack of curtains, asking if we had just moved in, but to us, the bright, open space decorated in soothing natural hues was a haven of tranquillity which was very special at the time. My mother passed on her love for antiques and vintage finds, as my sister and I often accompanied her on trips to thrift stores and flea markets. To this day, I treasure the dining chairs I purchased as a young girl on a trip to the island of Ameland.

Utrecht, the home city I return to after every trip, is a place of rich history and beauty. With its origins dating back over nine hundred years, it was built upon the remains of an ancient Roman fort. The city centre, with its canals, wharfs, and stone bridges, is a testament to its storied past. As I wander through its streets encircled by the Singel canal, I am constantly discovering new cityscapes, each one more breathtaking than the last. I know every nook and cranny of this city, every shop, every house. Though I often photograph Utrecht, I have never painted it. Yet, the colours and nature of the city are reflected in my artwork. Sometimes I sit by the canal, painting before rushing home to grab a pair of scissors to cut some wildflowers to bring back to my studio.

Home is a sanctuary, a place where the people I hold dearest, my children, husband, family, and friends gather. My home is a nest I have filled with straw and grass, not literally but metaphorically with the treasures I have collected over time. My interior reflects my passions, interests, and tastes, constantly evolving with me. It is never complete, leaving room for growth and change. My decor is whimsical, imperfect and unique, inspired by the beauty of nature. Nature teaches us to let go of perfection, as nothing is straight or symmetrical, and everything is subject to decay. With love and patience, we create a space that envelops us like a warm blanket, a place where my children often remark "How lovely it is here."

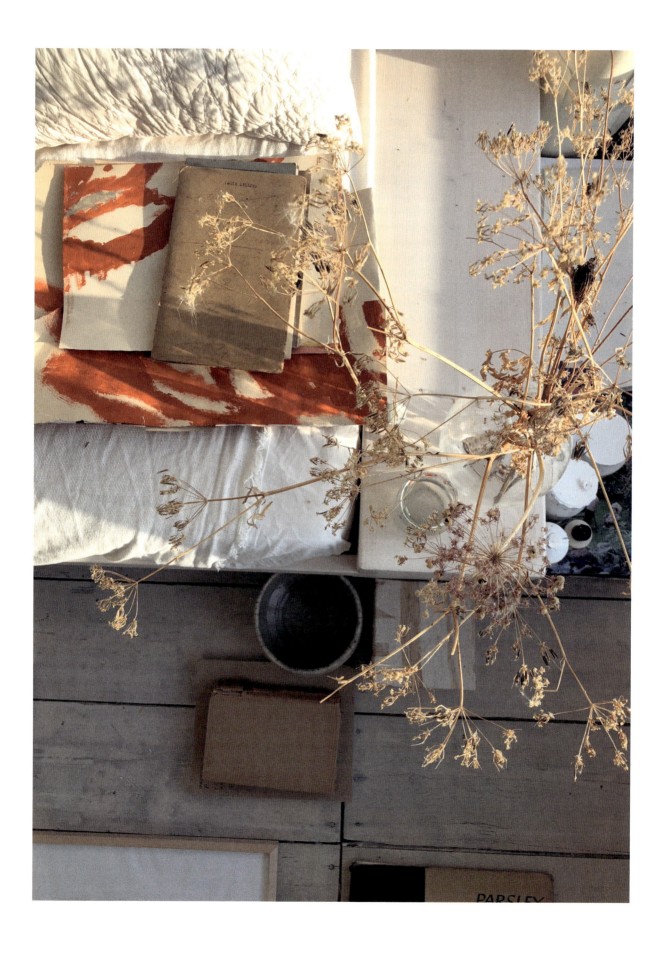

Morocco

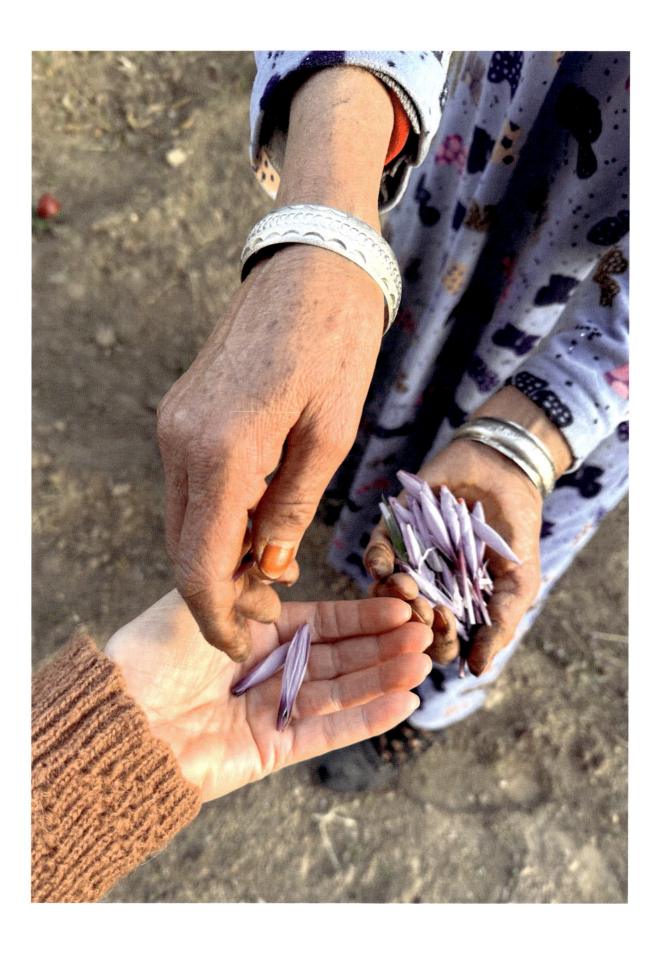

capturing the soul of Morocco

a love affair

Sitting in the back of an old Volkswagen, the sun is shining. The car bounces along a road which is pitted with potholes. I see the landscape fly by as if it were a fast-motion slideshow. In the front, my friend Nadia and her father are talking and laughing. I can't understand what they are saying but I hear the cadence of their voices and know that they are happy to be together again. Nadia's father is taking us to his favourite café in Tanger for breakfast, where we eat warm, freshly baked flatbread with *amlou*, an essentially liquid paste made from ground toasted almonds with honey and oil. I feel incredibly welcome. Nadia's father is proud and happy. He wants to show me his beautiful country, he says.

This initial journey marked the beginning of a love affair with the country, one that would captivate my heart over the ensuing years, enchanting me with its vibrant hues and evocative aromas. A land where I would revel in the radiance of its hospitality and the genuine warmth of its people. It soon emerged as a wellspring of inspiration for several artworks to come. The colours on my canvas deepened, imbued with a new-found intensity and warmth.

That first time, I immersed myself in all that Morocco had to offer, nature- and culture-wise. I pretended to be Moroccan, talking to everybody using hands, feet and my brushes. When I painted, people would often approach me and ask what I was doing, and a conversation would ensue naturally, sometimes with words, sometimes just with a sense of connection and a smile. I walked along the surf on the long, beautiful, vast beaches. Donkeys accompanied me. Rubbish was littered everywhere, and the sand was a sallow brown colour. This made no odds – it is what it is. This is how the people live here.

Years later, I find myself wandering through the bustling, sprawling open-air market, situated thirteen miles beyond Marrakech. More than a hundred stalls, tightly clustered together, sprawl across an expanse covering half a square mile. Narrow pathways wind between them, shaded by canvas coverings overhead. Donkeys and sheep are tethered nearby, while vendors clad in traditional attire linger amidst the lively exchange of bids and counterbids. The week's bounty is proudly displayed upon rugs and plastic sheets: an array of vegetables, potatoes, and various round root vegetables, alongside a cornucopia of fruits and nuts. Within a designated area, pottery, handmade doors, assorted used parts, wooden furniture and detergent are on offer, including the Moroccan black hamam soap. Fresh herbs and spices, boasting vivid hues, tantalise the senses, while the scent of sizzling meat over open fires intermingles at the back with the smoky aroma lingering in the air. Amidst this vibrant scene, men gather in mud huts, seated together on the floor, as they pour sugary-sweet tea into cups.

travelling teaches me to be adaptable

my diary is a collage of my artworks illustrating what I experienced that day

People from far and wide converge at this bustling market to sell and to stock up, predominantly men, with one veiled woman wearing a niqab passing through. Feeling the desire to blend in, I consider wearing a hijab to avoid standing out amidst the crowd. Opting to immerse myself fully in the present moment, I refrain from taking photographs, allowing the myriad of stories unfolding around me to fill my thoughts – the man selling his wares beneath an orange plastic sheet, the woman balancing a baby on her hip while offering an array of brightly coloured plastic tubs, and the barber deftly wielding his razor blade on a customer's throat. Amidst the bustling commerce, I am struck by the visible poverty – litter strewn about, and the peeling paint on the window frames of the mud huts. Beauty also dwells here. Absorbing the essence of the market, I gather fragments from the ground – a stone, a feather, a piece of cloth, a shard of earthenware pot, arranging them in my sketchbook to capture a palette of colours. Back home, I arrange these impressions onto paper or linen in my sketchbook, giving hues reminiscent of Morocco's weathered landscapes.

In Morocco, colours are imbued with a weathered, faded look, as if laundered all together by the elements. Yellows blend with pinks, evolving into sunset oranges under the shifting sunlight. Whitewashed browns and reds dominate inland, while coastal regions are adorned with whites, blues, and greens, reflecting the hues of beach and sea. The houses on the coast are whitewashed, sometimes with palm tree murals on the facades or a painted border around the doorframes. The sun and wind give the walls a weather-beaten look adding to the faded effect.

In Marrakech, colours take on a reddish-brown or warm-pink hue, simply more intense. This city is unfailingly different to any other city in Morocco. Wandering through the narrow walkways of the souk, I absorb the riot of colours – striped bags, traditional Berber rugs, scarves, long dresses, leather sandals, traditional slippers, tableware and brown bags filled to the brim with spices, without feeling compelled to purchase. Instead, I relish in observing the vibrant tapestry of daily life. In the early morning calm when the tourists are having their breakfast, I retreat to my favourite square, sketchbook on my lap in the shade of two palm trees to absorb the unfolding scenes – someone feeding chicken feet to stray cats, craftsmen getting into their vans for their day's work, an old man meandering by with an empty baggage cart. I sketch. Sometimes I make notes. Each moment is a vignette, a scene from a film. I capture them with pencil and paper, observing, Always observing. When I see something I like, my fingers tingle, a visceral reaction.

It is the people who make the country in the Berber village in the mountains, which I have visited several times now. It is predominantly the women with whom I feel a connection. Even though we cannot understand each other we intrinsically know what the other is saying. For a moment I become part of their lives. In the early morning, they knead the dough to make traditional flatbread. With a ball of dough under a cotton throw they walk to one of the communal stone ovens to get their bread baked. Every single day. The houses are simple square buildings with one door and one window. All rooms open onto a courtyard in the centre. The animals have their stalls here too – a cow with her calf, a donkey. There is a large loom in each house where the women

> I admire the women for their creativity, strength, self-sufficiency and their love for their land

weave rugs in the most beautiful colours. Some use traditional motifs, others freestyle and create unique patterns. The wool comes from their own sheep which graze on the edges of the mountains. The women wash, dye, comb and spin the precious wool themselves. When the rugs are finished they are washed and laid out to dry in the sun. At the edge of the village, a patchwork of hundreds of awe-inspiring, fairytale-like rugs in all colours, large and small, can be seen from far and wide.

I walk through the village and one of the women takes my arm and guides me inside her house. She serves me traditional Moroccan mint tea and homemade traditional Moroccan sweets. I show her pictures of The Netherlands. We laugh. She lets me take her photo, photos of her daughters, sisters and nieces. Their dresses and hijabs are brightly coloured and patterned with vibrant designs.

They make couscous – a formidable task. I help them to knead the dough. In one of the rooms, they bake the bread on a clay plate over an open fire. In the roof is a slit to ventilate the room, still, tears stream down my face from the pungent smoke. A glass of fresh buttermilk accompanies the couscous, along with mutton and vegetables. Everyone eats from the same tagine dish, and they all mix a few tablespoons of buttermilk in with the couscous. The Berber women giggle among themselves. Perhaps they perceive a woman travelling alone in a foreign land without her husband as unconventional. Maybe, like me, they simply enjoy being together. I feel at home here with these inspiring women.

The journey to the summer village, which is even higher up in the mountains, is breathtaking. The echoing barrenness is almost palpable. I can see for miles. There are rocks everywhere, the slopes are overgrown with low, prickly bushes. I lean out of the car and raise my arm whilst holding on to the car door with the other. My hair is whipping in the breeze. I laugh and scream with unbridled joy. Along the journey, we encounter a flock of sheep peacefully grazing through the arid landscape.

The village sits at the terminus of the road, nestled in a verdant valley. Constructed from large stones, the houses provide refuge for both humans and animals. With no access to electricity or running water, the community exists amidst fruit trees and small fields where saffron is harvested early autumn. Amidst the landscape, purple crocuses peek through, revealing the precious spice within their blossoms. Here, enveloped by nature, I feel a sense of purity, embraced by the community. It is here that I encounter Latifa, a young woman whose fragile beauty resonates deeply within me. I immortalise her face in a poignant portrait, capturing the essence of the mountains' hues. On the morning of our departure, Latifa holds me tightly in a deep embrace. I return her embrace, whispering softly in her ear that I will come back.

> I will always come back

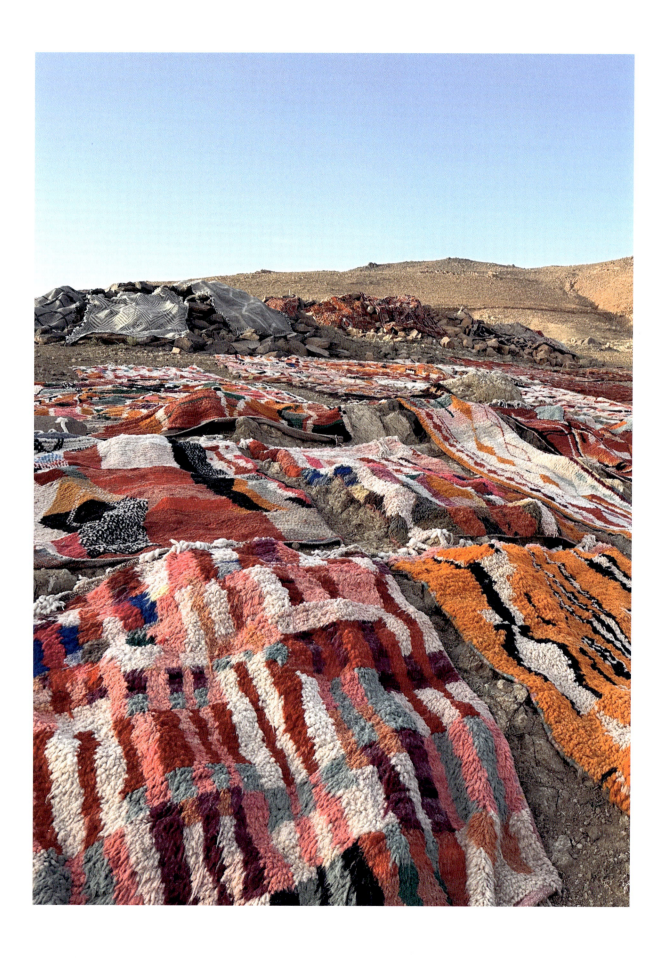

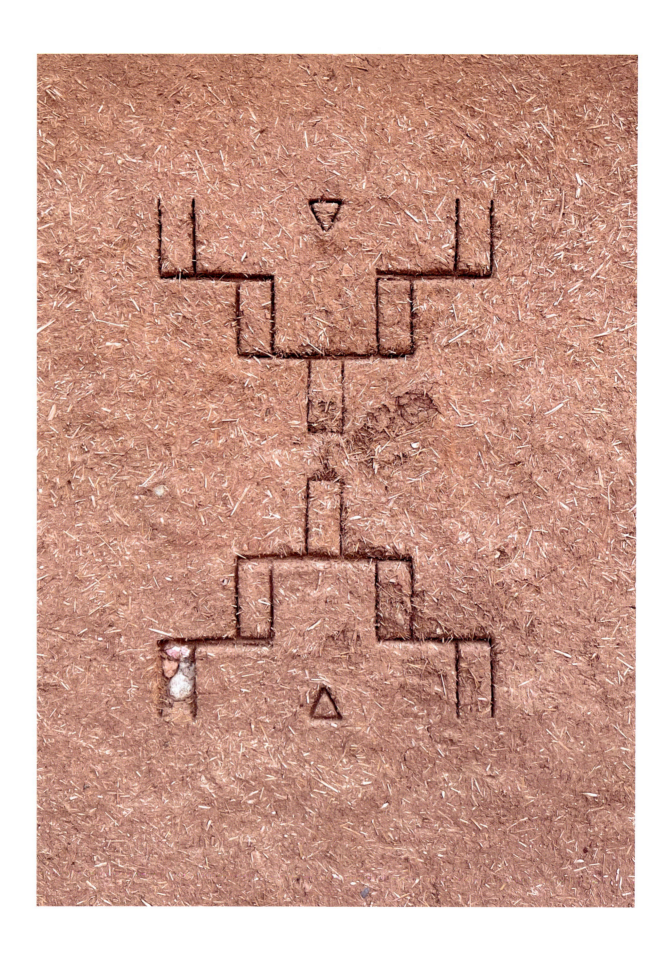

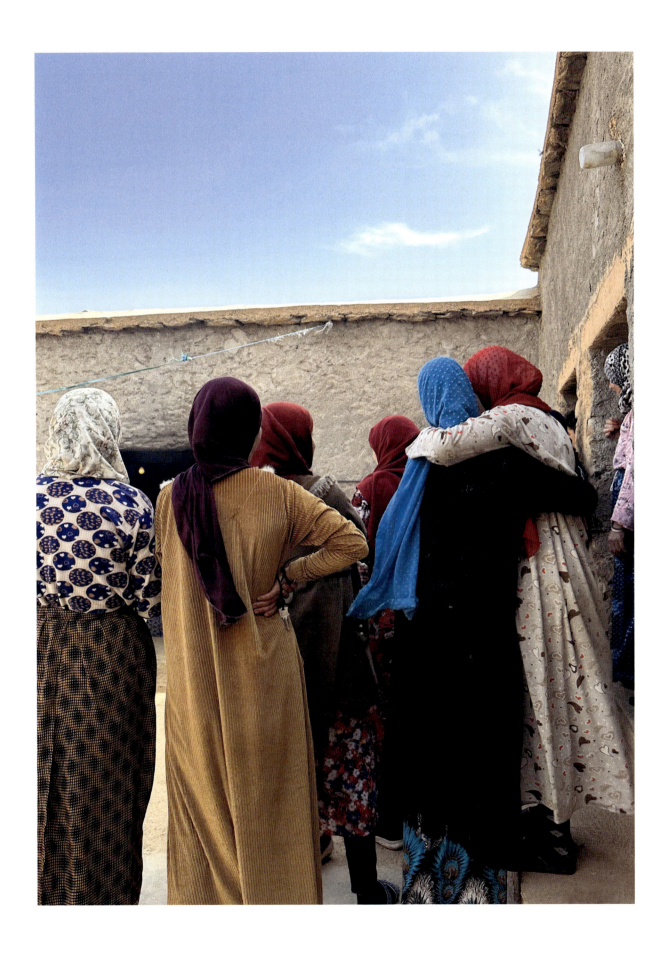

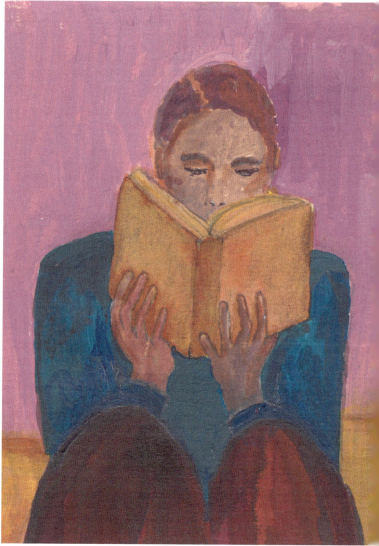

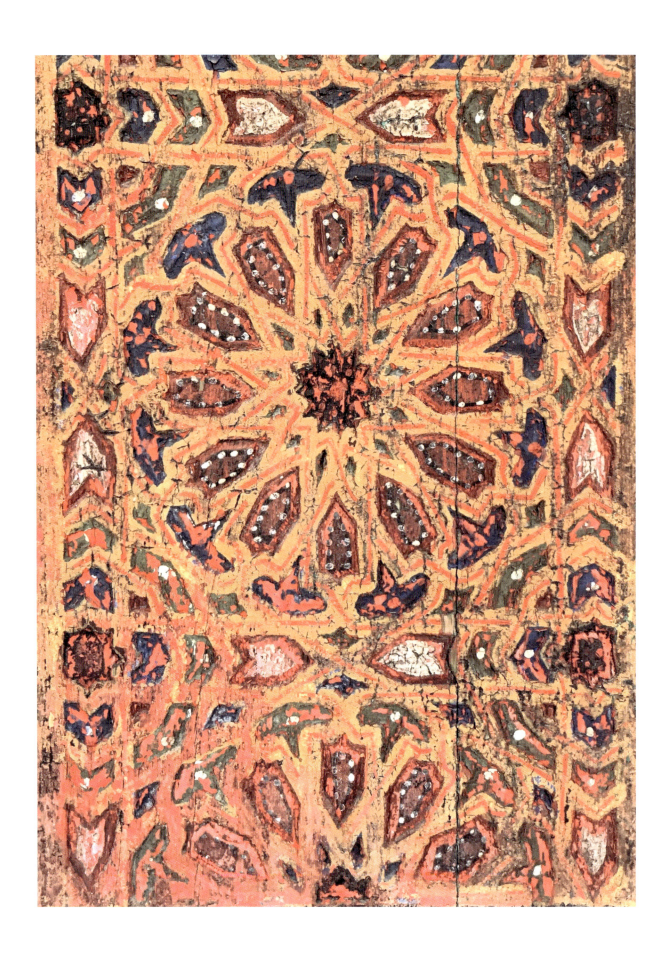

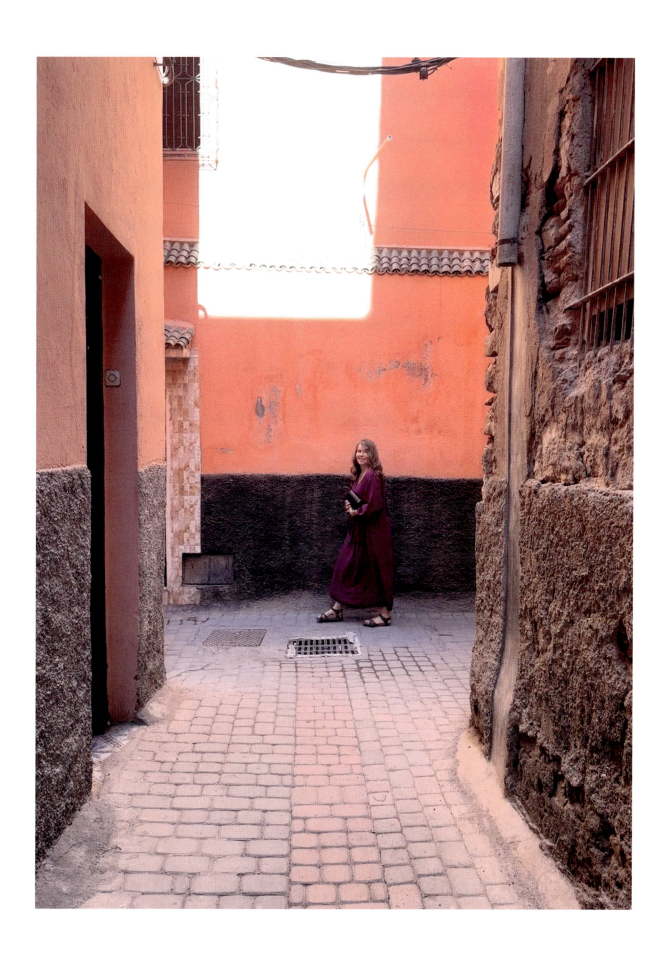

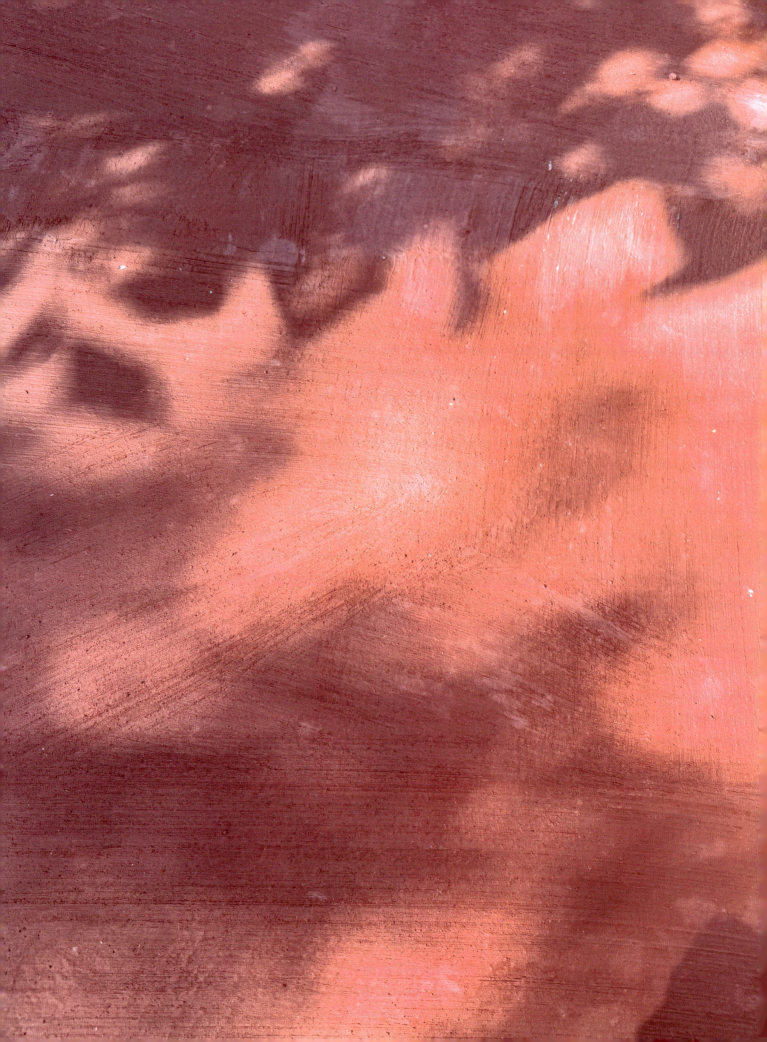

Germany

atelier Morgentau

hidden greenhouse in Brandenburg

As the sun sets, its last rays lengthen across the room, painting strips in a warm, golden light on the floor. A large canvas lies before me with more canvases scattered around. One hangs on the wall with only a few lines sketched upon it – the outline of a woman's form. I have just spent another blissful day in this enchanting old greenhouse, lost in my art. Only now do I realize that I have forgotten to eat. Time stands still when I paint, making everything around me fade into the background.

I paint and I dance
I dance and I paint

Nestled in a hidden garden surrounded by untamed beautiful nature lies my old friend – the greenhouse. The Brandenburg countryside with its authentic villages and rich history draws artists and creatives from Berlin into its serene embrace. They flock on summer weekends to swim, hike, paint, make music, and revel in the joys of life. Countless times have I gazed upon the beauty of the greenhouse, dreaming of the possibilities it might hold. And so when my wish was granted, I was overjoyed and I named it Atelier Morgentau – morning dew – for the promise of a new day filled with wonder.

The vast space in this studio allows for larger canvases, a contrast to the smaller format I am accustomed to in my studio. Before I arrived, I ventured to the fabric market in Utrecht where I gathered an array of fabrics to serve as my canvases. Unlike the daunting blankness of a ready-made canvas, fabrics offer a unique texture and character. I spent days preparing, my fingers itching with anticipation as I gathered painter's linen and other supplies. When I travel to paint, I bring everything I need to ensure no limitations hinder my creativity. I often work on multiple pieces simultaneously, sketching, setting them aside, and revisiting them days, weeks, or even months later. This process allows for a fresh perspective to be born and room for new ideas to flourish.

The architecture of this building strikes me with its graphic nature. The muntins in the large window frames inspire me to create abstract art. My brush strokes form lines and planes, shaping female figures on the canvas. A vintage chair catches my eye, its yellow hue seeping into my work. I take a walk, letting nature clear my mind and fill it with new images. I gather flowers and place them in an old jug, the sunlight dancing with their yellow petals. The door is open, the sound of birdsong filling the air. I am totally present in this moment of pure joy.

A sense of well-being overflows onto my canvas. The freedom is exhilarating. In the solitude of my studio, I am at one with my muse. Everything falls into perfect harmony, and my art takes on a life of its own.

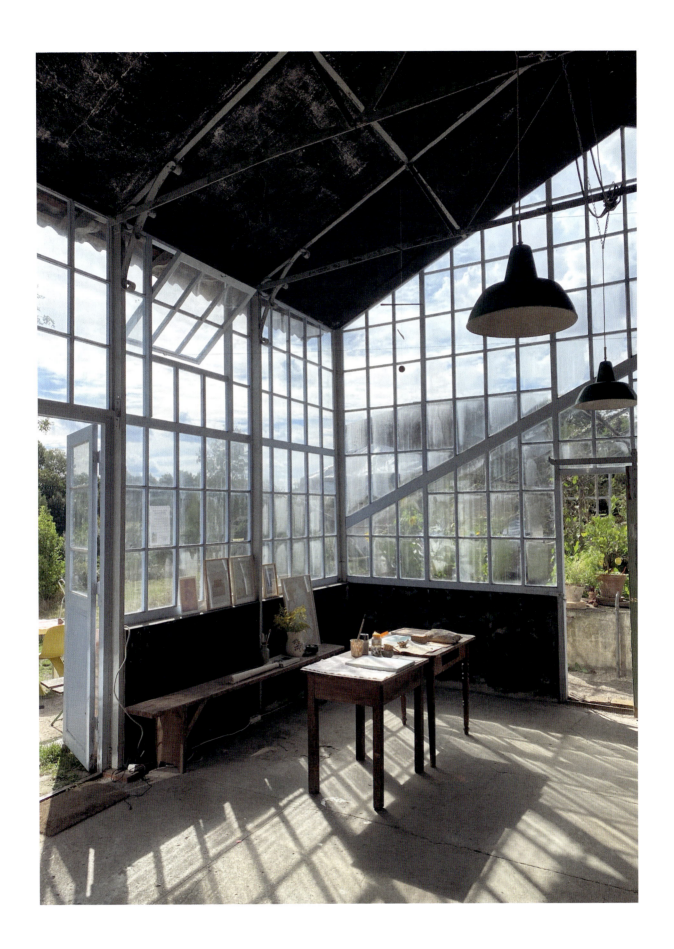

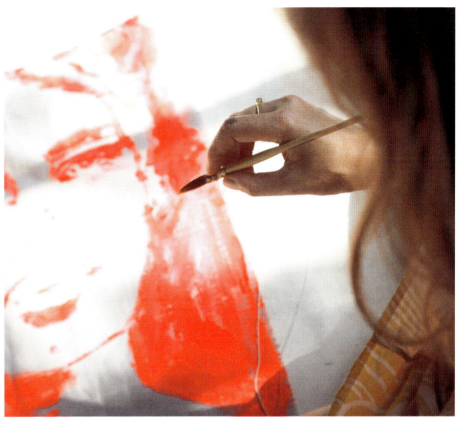
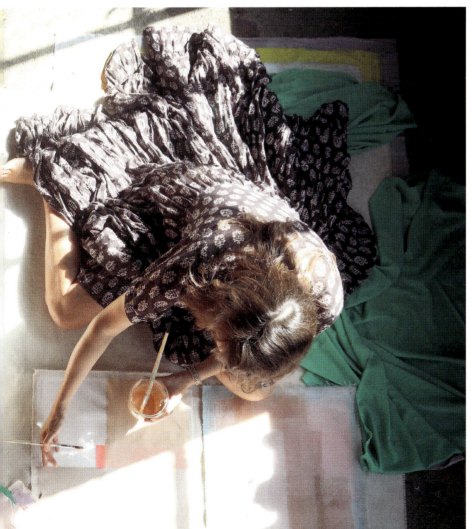

Australia

Tasmania

Lettes Bay– hideaway on the water

Perched upon the bench before the grand window, my gaze is drawn to the breathtaking expanse of Lettes Bay. The wooden jetty extends into the water, a steadfast companion to the bobbing boats of the fishermen who braved the waters yesterday. The view is awe-inspiring, the vastness humbling. The wind whips, sending grey clouds scurrying across the sky. Today I am content to remain within the cosy confines of Captain's Rest. The fire crackles merrily in the wood-burning stove, my paper and brushes at the ready. I shall spend the day painting and sketching, capturing the beauty before me.

The cottage is an old wooden fishing cottage lovingly restored to perfection by its Australian owner, Sarah. The front facade boasts large windows that stretch across its width, offering breathtaking views of the water and sky from every vantage point in the house. The picturesque scenery, akin to a framed painting, changes with every passing moment as the light dances and plays with the colours of the landscape. I can sit in this light for hours. One day it can shift from bright blue to dark grey and everything in between. As the day breaks, the soft quacking of the resident ducks, fondly referred to as 'the girls' by Sarah, can be heard. This charming abode is a true gem.

We drive for hours from Tasmania's capital, Hobart, along Australia's southern coast, surrounded by pristine wilderness. Our destination is the serene Lettes Bay on the island's west coast. Life here is pure and unadorned. Our cabin, a majestic haven, has been decorated with care. The furnishings are an eclectic mix of custom-designed, handcrafted, and vintage pieces. Old oil paintings adorn the walls, creating an effortless perfection. Handmade pottery graces the kitchen while the plush, high bed is dressed in nature-inspired linens in rich greens and browns. Each evening, we stoke the wood-burning stove, embracing the simplicity of life here.

We journey to a picturesque bay near Strahan where unique flora flourishes. We espy star-shaped grass balls which, when caught by a gust of wind, release their hold and tumble across the beach like enormous arachnids. It is a breathtaking sight. Later, while perusing a flea market in Daylesford, I chance upon a book about native plants and learn that this particular dune grass is known as spinifex or hairy spinifex – an amusing name for such an elegant plant.

there is nowhere else I would rather be

Every day I immerse myself in my paintings, filling my sketchbooks with the natural hues of greens, browns, sand and water. Here in this place of purity there are no distractions, only the raw elements of wind, water, air and earth. I sit at my wooden table gazing out the window, observing and revelling in the beauty before me.

Bruny Island

a pristine pearl at the end of the world

We journey through Hobart and make our way to the southeast of Tasmania, eager to uncover Bruny Island's secrets. As the afternoon sun begins to set, we stumble upon a curious sight – two vintage cream-coloured refrigerators by the side of the road. Intrigued, we open one of the doors and are delighted to find freshly baked bread inside. What a wonderful surprise on an island with only one general store which is not always open! We continue our journey along the small road, encouraged that we are on the right path, and soon arrive at our cabin on Sheepwash Bay where we will sleep tonight. The view is nothing short of breathtaking.

As the sun rises the next morning, the delicious aroma of freshly baked bread fills the air. I walk outside and follow the scent to a quaint stone building nestled behind our hut. Smoke billows from the chimney. There I find John, the mastermind behind Bruny Bakery. He is the one responsible for stocking the fridges at the start of the road with his delectable homemade sourdough bread. I savour a warm slice, slathered with homemade jam and butter, as we sip coffee and chat. John shares his love for bread making and how Bruny Island captured his heart and became his home.

On this island nature is ever-present, sometimes in the extreme. As I wake up at night and stroll towards the outdoor lavatory, the beam of my flashlight illuminates the night, revealing dozens of tiny, gleaming eyes peering at me from the shrubbery. My initial shock subsides as my vision adjusts to the darkness and I am greeted by the sight of curious wallabies, watching my every move.

Every evening as the sun sets we gather on the pebbled shore to light a fire. We forage for oysters and roast vegetables, sometimes even grilling a fish we caught ourselves. I lose track of time as I observe the bustling marine life in the tide pools nestled between the rocks. Sun-patterned shells scuttle across the ocean floor, while yellow-green seaweed dances in the current. As the stones dry out and the seaweed basks in the sun, it transforms into a new spectacle. I capture this enchanting world through my lens, preserving its beauty in photographs.

I watch the sun-patterned shells scuttle across the ocean floor

I gather treasures from the earth: stones, shells, feathers, leaves, including beautiful eucalyptus leaves in faded pastel hues, and arrange them into intricate compositions. These serve as the foundation for my drawings and paintings. I capture the essence of the bay and the distant mountains. With nature as my constant companion, I am never at a loss for inspiration. The beauty of this place is boundless, ever-changing with each passing moment.

On a bright morning, we journey to the Cape Bruny Lighthouse, where the snow-white structure stands tall, illuminating the edge of the world like a guiding light. As I stand at the base of the lighthouse, perched atop a mountain, the fierce winds blow and I feel as if I could fall off the edge of the earth.

This enchanting island has captured my heart, filling each day with awe and wonder.

Daylesford and Melbourne

bathed in light

As I stroll through the streets of Daylesford, an old gold mining village nestled in the heart of Southern Australia, the warm sunlight illuminates my path as I follow my shadow. The rolling countryside dotted with vineyards and lavender fields transports me to the idyllic South of France, but the presence of koalas and kangaroos brings me back down to Australian earth. I am enamoured by the town's Edwardian architecture with its intricate balustrade carvings and the cornices on the verandas. Every front garden is a picture to behold, bursting with lush greenery and colourful blooms.

My passion for architecture and design was kindled during my formative years. Perched on a stool with my feet dangling, I would sit beside my father, an architect, and watch in awe as he worked at his large drawing table. The intricacies of floor plans, the beauty of front views and the artistry of house sketches captivated me. I remember the sound of graphite on sandpaper as he sharpened his pencils with a special ruler lined with narrow strips of sandpaper. With the gentle strokes of his pencil, he brought his visions to life on the chalk paper clamped securely to the angled drawing table. Each line was then traced in ink, and any mistakes were carefully erased with the scrape of a knife. As I grew older, I was entrusted with the task of selecting colours and materials, and I often accompanied him to the construction site. It was awe-inspiring to witness the transformation of a simple sketch into a tangible structure. I couldn't help but be captivated by the restorations of the old buildings in Elburg's centre. But what truly fascinated me was the story behind their restoration. Before any work could begin, archaeologists would excavate the soil, uncovering a treasure trove of artifacts – pottery, stones and other ancient relics.

As I meander through each street of Daylesford, I take in every detail, from the houses to the gardens. My eyes are drawn upwards to the sky, where the clouds paint hues from pale pink to orange in the setting sun. I commit every detail to memory, creating a tapestry of warmth and colour in my memory bank.

my father inspired my love for architecture and design

Our abode is a stunning creation, designed and decorated by my friend, Lynda Gardner. Her unique style blends the old with the new, weaving a tapestry of natural hues and materials. She uniquely juxtaposes textures and design elements from rustic to modern, whilst masterfully balancing light and dark. We share a passion for travel, flea markets, and the charm of time-worn objects which add layers to an interior. She weaves tales through her interior designs, blending vintage furnishings and art with exquisite household items. We are both impassioned treasure hunters. Once, in my hometown Utrecht, we embarked on a quest to explore its antique shops. Each store and its display window were a treasure trove, revealing new wonders with every visit.

the interior feels as though it has always been this way, effortlessly perfect

Night has fallen as I step back into our house. I light candles. This morning, we were greeted by the sun's gentle rays as we stirred from our slumber between the soft linen sheets. The house, with its simple barn-like structure, is bathed in light that pours in through the grand windows, salvaged from an old schoolhouse. My eyes wander over the vintage furnishings, the art that adorns the walls, and the greenery that thrives in large antique baskets and pots. The interior feels as though it has always been this way, effortlessly perfect. Casual.

Australia's light captivates me. It is akin to gazing through a pane of unblemished glass. At times, it takes on an enigmatic, gentle quality.

Our journey takes us on to Melbourne where we stay at the White Room, a beautiful studio designed by Lynda, located in an old mattress factory in the Fitzroy district. Lynda's influence is evident on all levels with stacks of books and intriguing trinkets from flea markets from across the globe. The space is brimming with intricate details and unexpected treasures – a feast for the eyes. Beyond the French doors I step into a secluded courtyard garden, its walls draped in green ivy. Here, amidst the tranquillity, the hustle and bustle of the city fade into the distance.

Melbourne has captured my heart with its uninhibited atmosphere, tropical landscapes, serene ocean, and quaint Federation-style houses adorned with terracotta tiles, gabled roofs, intricate woodwork, and delicate cast-iron lacework details on the verandas reminiscent of elaborate crochet patterns. My friend Ursula, along with her husband and children, resides in Elwood on the border of St. Kilda, a picturesque corner of Melbourne.

Together, we stroll down every street, admiring each house and garden. The area is abundant with stunning native flora, evoking memories of Bandung. Melbourne captures my heart thanks to Ursula. Her tales of growing up in the city, the exhibitions we visit, and the beauty she introduces me to all contribute to my love for the place.

As we bid farewell to Australia and journey back home, my mind and sketchbooks overflow with countless images, drawings and memories.

France

the south of France

capturing the beauty of flowers

As I drive along a long road, I find myself surrounded by tall plane trees lining the avenue, the sunlight dappling between the leaves creating a veritable juxtaposition of light and shadow. Perched atop a hill in the distance, the village of Neffiès beckons me closer.

From the moment our paths crossed, Yvonne and I had an instant connection. Yvonne, originally from Sweden, and her husband run a *chambre d'hôtes* nestled in a petite French village, housed in a traditional sandstone building dated 1857. My room boasts views of sprawling vineyards, with the majestic Pyrenees and their snow-capped peaks in the distance. As I turn my gaze to the interior, I am enveloped by the warmth of my surroundings – the sandy hues of the embroidered linen bedding, the intricate patterns of the original floor tiles in shades of blue and soft orange.

Yvonne's passion for French brocante style and natural materials is evident throughout her home. The decor features an artful blend of jute, linen, wool, and cotton, combining the elegance of French design with the simplicity of Scandinavian style. She has gathered a collection of antique linen and hemp fabrics for me which she has dyed using natural, homemade dyes made from kitchen scraps such as onion skins and herbs.

With textile paint and ink, I bring to life the beauty of wildflowers on the canvas of antique linen. Later, Yvonne transforms these painted fabrics into cushion covers and wall hangings. Our collaboration breathes new life into our creations, each piece telling its own unique story. The joy of creating together is priceless.

Yvonne leads me through her favourite antique shops, each one filled with treasures and trinkets. In one, an open cupboard reveals a trove of textiles: quilted blankets and curtains adorned with the most exquisite floral prints, all a source of inspiration. I begin to imagine how I might translate this French romance into a fresh creation. My brushstrokes are loose and fluid, capturing the essence of the flowers rather than their precise details. I retain their natural hues – the warm red and vibrant pink of the bougainvillea, the blue of the cornflowers. On a piece of antique tissue paper I create a painting, incorporating dried flower petals onto the canvas and painting in more petals.

As the sun sets, we savour a glass of organic wine on the terrace, basking in the warmth of the day's final rays. We raise our glasses in a toast to our love for France.

la vie est belle

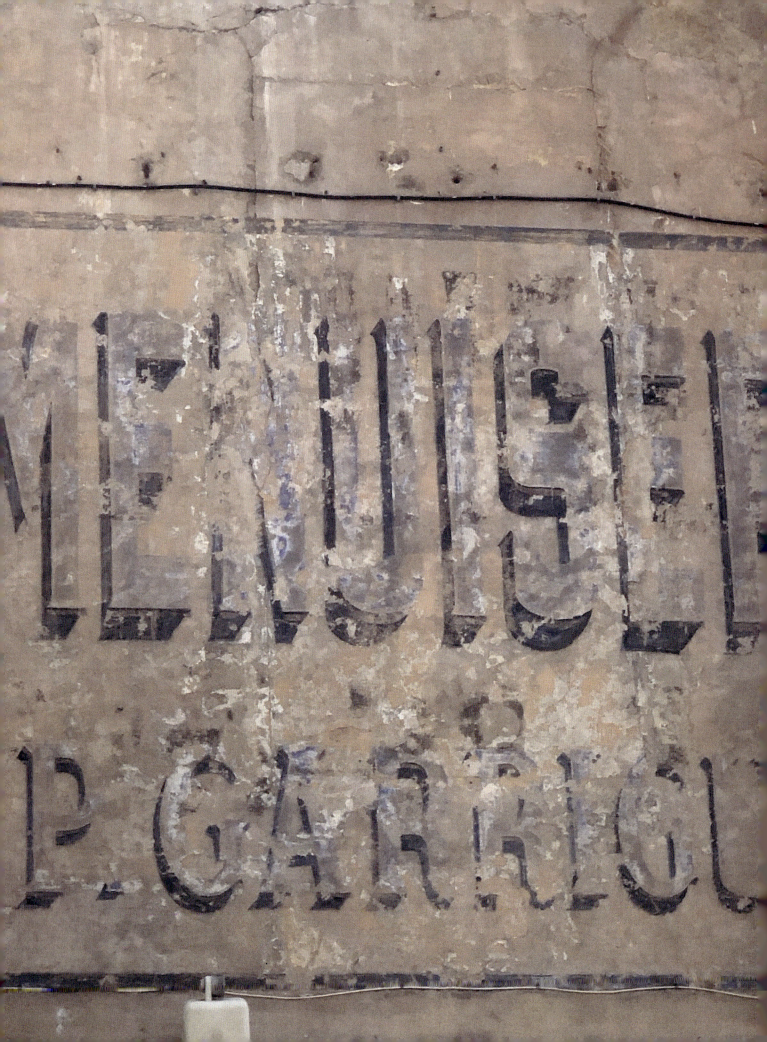

the Dordogne

painting in Emmy's chateau

Walking barefoot towards my bedroom, a whirlwind of dust rises with each step. The wooden floor, smooth and warm, soothes my feet. I have spent the entire morning in the studio. Bright rays of sunlight sneak through the cracks of the closed shutters. The night before, the rain had pounded against the windows, rousing me from my slumber. The room was intermittently illuminated by flashes of lightning followed by the roar of thunder. I had risen from my bed to secure the shutters. Once back under the covers, I felt cocooned in safety.

I am awakened from my slumber by the warm rays of the sun. The aroma of freshly baked croissants and rich coffee wafts through the air. Emmy welcomes me with a hug and beckons me to join her at the table. I relish the melody of her voice as she regales me with tales of the castle, her pride and joy. When she first acquired it, the grand structure was in a state of disrepair, neglected and forgotten. But with determination and love, Emmy is restoring it to its former glory, one room at a time. She shares her joy with me, allowing me to use the grand room at the front of the castle as my studio.

My mind wanders back to my first visit to this enchanting place. I meandered through the labyrinth of rooms, each one holding its own secrets. As I gazed upon the wooden rafters, a diminutive snowy owl took flight onto a beam, its wings a blur of white. Bats flitted about, and abandoned wasp nests clung to the walls. It was as if I had embarked on a journey through time. My fingers traced the faded wallpaper and crumbling stucco, each layer telling its own story. I felt as if I were a princess in a fairy-tale castle, waiting to stumble upon the ghosts of its past inhabitants adorned in their flowing gowns.

Emmy and I embark on a quest to find the most exquisite fabrics, dishware and furnishings to adorn the castle from car boot sales. Each chamber is to be uniquely decorated. As I peruse Emmy's collection of books on fashion from the eighteenth and nineteenth centuries, I am filled with inspiration. I paint elegant women in rustling gowns. Sunlight pours into the studio through the expansive windows. French doors open onto a platform with a staircase descending to the lawn, where the withered grass has grown tall. I lose myself in a fantasy world, imagining myself as the lady of the castle reclining on a plush canapé sofa, surrounded by flickering candlelight.

each layer of the faded wallpaper tells its own story

With my eyes closed, I flit through the garden of my childhood home. The blades of grass brush against my skin, tickling my bare ankles. I am ten years old and my sister and I have been constructing grand castles from cardboard and paper, whispering secrets in a language only we understand. We fashion everything with our own hands, from paper dresses to makeshift shoes using old newspaper and paper. Inside, our creativity knows no bounds. We erect entire villages, complete with dolls' houses and houseboats in the living room. Old rolls of wallpaper become canvases for our art. Our mother nurtures our creativity, providing us with all the materials we need to bring our imagination to life. A sudden wave of emotion washes over me, and tears stream down my face. How I miss my sister.

the hours flow seamlessly as I surrender to the enchantment of days gone by

Emmy is an ambitious dreamer who follows the whims of her heart. With no set path, she embraces the unknown. When her sons come to visit we gather around the table al-fresco, sharing stories and laughter as we dine surrounded by bowls of food. The young men are unguarded, their enthusiasm infectious. I revel in their headstrong nature, their refusal to see obstacles. And every day I paint. The dusty windows of my studio cast a beautiful light, embracing the imperfect and leaving room for the imagination. As night falls, I see myself reflected in the glass.

France entrances me with its vibrant colours, ethereal light, and flowers. The sandstone houses exude a rustic charm while the markets brim with treasures – bric-a-brac, antique furniture, and exotic fabrics. I scour the stalls for old French linen, the perfect canvas for my art. And I cherish the banana tree paper that I still have from Bandung, careful to let its unique texture and colours shine through my paintings. I lose myself in the creative process, sketching, painting, and drawing, as memories and musings inspire my work.

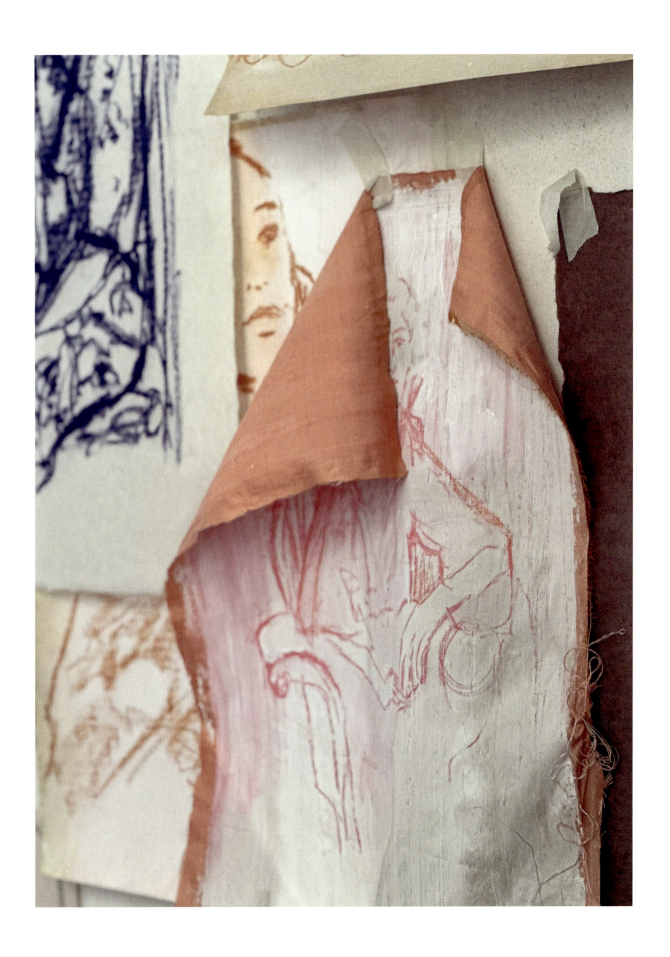

my favourite places

I love beautiful places. Places where the love and care put into them are visible, where there is time for each other, where I love to take my dearest people. These special places I'm happy to share with you.

Indonesia
Elina Keramik
Elina Farida
Bandung, Java
elinakeramik.co.id
@elina.keramik

The Netherlands
Utrecht
Swaak 1892, art supplies
Oudegracht 195

Keek, restaurant
Oudegracht 362

Daen's, restaurant
Korte Minrebroederstraat 13-17

Fabric market
Breedstraat, Saturday morning

Flower market
Janskerkhof, Saturday

Biologic food market
Vredenburgplein, Friday

De Witte Eenhoorn, brocante
Oudegracht 300

De Oude Pijpenlade, brocante
Oudegracht 199

Around Utrecht
De Veldkeuken, restaurant
Koningslaan 11, Bunnik

Piet Jonker, architectural antiques
Rijksstraatweg 23, Baambrugge

Morocco
I co-organise creative retreats
bookings via:
Liefde voor Marokko
Caroline Cornelisse-Kuiper
liefdevoormarokko.nl
@liefdevoormarokko

Tour guide Morocco
Jalil Aitoufkir
@morocco_wanderlust_concept

Riad Dar Palm
Caroline Cornelisse-Kuiper
Marrakech
liefdevoormarokko.nl
@riad_dar_palm

Riad UP
Elza Bauza
Marrakech
riadup.com
@riad_up

Germany
Berlin
Café im Literaturhaus, restaurant
Fasanenstrasse 23

Cookies Cream, restaurant
Behrenstrasse 55

Woodstock, fabric store
Hufelandstrasse 27

Flea market
Arkonaplatz, Sunday

Around Berlin
Gut Boltenhof
Lindenallee 14, Fuerstenberg-Havel
@gut_boltenhof

B&B Pfarrhaus Recknitz
Recknitz 7, 18276 Plaaz
@theoldpriesthouse

Australia
Captain's Rest
Sarah Andrews
Lettes Bay, Strahan, Tasmania
captainsrest.com
@captainsrest

Sheepwash Bay
John Bullock
Bruny Island, Tasmania
sheepwashbay.com
@sheepwashbay

Room + Board, The White house,
and The White room
Lynda Gardener
Daylesford & Melbourne, Victoria
lyndagardener.com
@lynda.gardener

France
La Belle Vue
Yvonne Tenninge
Neffiès
labellevue.se
@labellevueneffies

B&B Château des Chauvaux
Emmy Postma
Douzillac
chateaudeschauvaux.com
@chateauchauvaux

made with love

colophon

Concept, artwork and photography
Tiny de Vries, tinystories.nl

Designs cover and interior
Tiny de Vries & Bea Oostenenk
Atelier Oost, atelieroost.nl

Storytelling
Flory Hartog
@studiofloryhartog

Translation
Bryony Kate Howard
in-situ.eu.com

Copy editing
Barbara Luijken, Marijke Overpelt

First print, 2024

© 2024
Uitgeverij Terra is part of
Uitgeverij Lannoo nv
P.O. Box 23202
1100 DS Amsterdam
The Netherlands

terra@lannoo.nl
lannoo.com

f terrapublishing
 terrapublishing

ISBN 9789401446747
NUR 450

additional images

Nikki van de Poel
pages 40, 41, 42, 47, 48, 51, 52, 53
Satellite June, analoge photography,
satellitejune.com, @satellitejune

Sebastian Semmer
pages 154, 156, 157, 158, 159, 160,
161, 162, 163, 164, 165, 166, 167
Foto Semmer, foto-semmer.de

Yvonne Tenninge
page 216
La Belle Vue, labellevue.se,
@labellevueneffies

artwork in webshop

All artwork is painted by Tiny de Vries
Art prints are available at tinystories.nl

Cover		Bay view
page	2	Wildflowers
page	8	Frangipani flower
page	20	Bali
page	23	Follow rivers
page	32	Listen to the silence
page	37	Chocolate flowers, Korean flowers
page	40	Berber girl
page	43	L'amour
page	44	Whispers from the woods
page	50	A moment in time
page	57	Pendientes de flecos
page	60	Sakura, Dreaming of palmtrees, In a field of flowers
page	61	Tiny little things
page	63	Fleurs Japonaises
page	69	I love you, De paysage, Korean flowers
page	74	Coral & chocolate
page	93	Berber girl
page	106	Serein
page	118	Bay view
page	124	Livre
page	128	Citrons à l'indigo
page	132	Lemon & raspberry pie
page	136	Dans les rues de Marrakech
page	140	Belle matinée
page	148	Palm
page	151	Belles fleurs
page	158	L'amour and Verte
page	166	Nongkrong
page	172	Let's go on an adventure
page	175	Little bay
page	190	Sultry skies
page	193	De paysage
page	200	As free as the ocean
page	205	Loving embrace
page	206	Ochre
page	208	The songs of trees
page	214	French roses
page	221	Moonflowers
page	226	Blue moon
page	233	Blue eyes
page	239	Lumière dorée
page	247	Wild flowers
page	253	L'amour and Sakura

thank you

Alexa, Gesa, Jennifer, Laetitia,
Marie-Alix, Merry, Tim and Roland

**Room + Board, The White house,
The White room**
Lynda Gardener
Daylesford & Melbourne, Victoria, Australia
lyndagarder.com, @lynda.gardener

Captain's Rest
Sarah Andrews
Lettes Bay, Strahan, Tasmania, Australia
captainsrest.com, @captainsrest

Sheepwash Bay
John Bullock
Sheepwash Bay, Tasmania, Australia
sheepwashbay.com, @sheepwashbay

B&B Château des Chauvaux
Emmy Postma
Douzillac, France
chateaudeschauvaux.com
@chateauchauvaux

La Belle Vue
Yvonne Tenninge
Neffiès, France
labellevue.se, @labellevueneffies

Elina Keramik
Elina Farida
Bandung, Java, Indonesia
elinakeramik.co.id, @elina.keramik

Riad Dar Palm
Caroline Cornelisse-Kuiper
Marrakech, Morocco
liefdevoormarokko.nl
@riad_dar_palm

Riad Up
Elsa Bauza
Marrakech, Morocco
riadup.com, @riad_up

All rights reserved. No part of this publication may be reproduced and/or made public by means of printing, photocopying, microfilm or by any other means, without the prior written permission of the publisher. This edition has been compiled with the utmost care. Neither the maker nor the publisher, however, is liable for any damage as a result of any inaccuracies and/or omissions in this publication.